P9-BIR-943

Knowing Beans about
COFFEE

New Cooking & Brewing Ideas

by
Joan Korenblit & Kathie Janger

AMERICAN
★ COOKING ★
GUILD

Boynton Beach, Florida

Dedication
The authors thank the many individuals who gave their time, advice, and information, or who donated their taste buds on our behalf. Special gratitude to our publisher; to Dan Cox and Suzanne J. Brown; and to our families—particularly our spouses, Mike and Steve— for enduring our many experiments and for their love and support.

Joan Bravo Korenblit and Kathleen Janger

Acknowledgments
—Cover Design and Layout by Pearl & Associates, Inc.
—Cover Photo by Burwell and Burwell
—Editorial Assistance from Dan Cox and Ellen Jordan
—Illustrations by Loel Barr
—typesetting and Layout by BOSS Publication Production Services

Revised Edition 1997
Copyright © 1985 by Joan Korenbilt and Kathie Janger
All rights reserved.
Printed in U.S.A.
ISBN 0-942320-17-4

More…Quick Recipes for Creative Cooking!
The American Cooking Guild's *Collector's Series* includes over 30 popular cooking topics such as Barbeque, Breakfast & Brunches, Chicken, Cookies, Hors d' Oeuvres, Seafood, Tea, Coffee, Pasta, Pizza, Salads, Italian and many more. Each book contains more than 50 selected recipes. For a catalog of these and many other full sized cookbooks, send $1 to the address below and a coupon will be included for $1 off your first order.

Cookbooks Make Great Premiums!
The American Cooking Guild has been the premier publisher of private label and custom cookbooks since 1981. Retailers, manufacturers, and food companies have all chosen The American Cooking Guild to publish their premium and promotional cookbooks. For further information on our special markets programs please contact the address.

The American Cooking Guild
3600-K South Congress Avenue
Boynton Beach, FL 33426

CONTENTS

Introduction 5
The Basics 6
    The Beans 6
    Decaffeination 7
    The Roast 7
    The Blends 8
    The Grind 8
    The Brew 8
    The Taste 9
    The Aroma 9
Basic Coffee Concentrate 9

BEVERAGES
Jamaican Egg Nog 10
Café au Lait 11
Coffee Ice Cream Soda 11
Chocolate Coffee Ice Cream Soda 11
Coffee Concentrate Café au Lait 12
Irish Coffee 12
Camper's Java 12
Café Caribe 13
Café Brûlot 13
Easy Espresso and Cappuccino 14
Caffè Latte 14
Hot Buttered Coffee 15
Italian Coffee 15
Coffee Royale 16
Coffee Frappe 16
Choco-Mocha Smoothie 16

ENTREES AND MORE
Seafood Quiche 17
Chicken Teriyaki 18
Coffee Glazed Ham 18
Lasagna 19
Coffee Tomato Sauce 19
Beef Curry 20
Chop Suey with Pork 21
Peppercorn Chicken 21
Tandoori Chicken 22
Crêpes Divan 23
Pepper Steak 25
Souvlaki (Greek Sandwich) 26
Minty Lamb Stew 27
Veal Paprika 28

Moussaka 29
Tomato Chutney 30
Mexican Dip..30
Tomato Aspic...31
Maple Walnut Baked Beans 31

DESSERTS

Apricot Brownies...34
Chocolate Coffee Pie..35
Coffee Chiffon Cake 36
Coffee Parfaits...37
Mocha Ice Cream 37
Viennese Cinnamon Date Nut Bread 38
Festive Coconut Balls...38
Fruit Creme/Sherbet 39
Chocolate Peanut Butter Fondue 39
Kahlua Cream 40
Pastry Crust...40
Tiramisu 41
Baklava 42
Biscotti 43
Fudge Sauce...44
Coffee Lemon Bars 44
Pecan Praline Bread Pudding 45
Coffee Coconut Mousse Pie 46
Mint Mocha Raspberry Bombe...46
Kiwi Lime Pie 47
Cashew Coconut Crust 47
Strawberry Coffee Cheesecake 48
Graham Cracker Crust 48
Mocha Torte...49

ESPECIALLY FOR ENTERTAINING

How to Conduct a Coffee Tasting at Home...............................50
Cold Drink Coffee Bar..52
Hot Drink Coffee Bar 53
Taco Bar 54
Espresso Bar 54

APPENDIX

Coffee Brewing...55
Coffee Accessories 58
Java Jive—Espresso Glossary..59
Liqueurs, Alcohol and Extracts..60
Where It's Grown 61
Supplementary Reading List..63

INTRODUCTION

It wakes us up in morning, invigorates us at midday, and relaxes us at night. Coffee. The perfect beverage. Anytime. Any occasion.

Espresso at a sidewalk cafe, Irish coffee at Fisherman's Wharf in San Francisco, a chipped mug of java at that wonderful diner you discovered, the unpronounceable concoction you tried in Mexico—these are special moments intertwined with coffee. Mr. Coffee is proud of its role in the evolution of this internationally adored beverage. Mr. Coffee introduced the first automatic drip coffeemaker over 25 years ago, and thereby enhanced the brewing process by eliminating the bitter taste and long brew times of its predecessor, the percolator. The result—a great-tasting cup of coffee every time!

Knowing Beans About Coffee is a collection of recipes and facts to help you better understand coffee terms and descriptions related to coffee. It is a how-to manual for making the familiar, the unusual, and the surprising—from ice cream to barbecue sauce. We have also provided product information, brewing techniques, household hints and instant flavor tips.

So refill your breakfast cup and relax while you pore over the pages that follow. There's bound to be something here to tickle your fancy—and use up the coffee you've already brewed!

THE BASICS

If you've mastered the complexities of wine and grapes—the origins, soil, climate, and bottling—then you have an idea of the components that comprise the complicated commodity of coffee. Advertisements and spokespersons are likening the coffee industry to the centuries-old traditions of enology: if you know the grapes, then you know the wine; so then, you should know the beans in order to know the coffee.

It is not our purpose to be the complete resource on coffee. There are a number of fine, exhaustively researched volumes on the subject, which are identified in the Supplementary Reading List. But it is our desire to inform you of the basics so that your next experience with coffee beans doesn't leave you scrambling to understand even the most elementary coffee jargon. Here goes.

THE BEANS

There are two major species of coffee: *arabica* and *robusta.* Arabica trees are usually grown in altitudes above 2–3,000 feet; robusta trees grow best below 2,000 feet. Coffee trees flourish in rich, moist soil, the best of which is composed of leafmold and volcanic rock or ash. Thus the term "mountain or high grown" coffee has been used to denote superior coffee. Coffee grown at higher altitudes provides a brew that is lighter and more delicate; lower altitudes produce coffee with fuller-bodied, harsher flavor. Robustas are less expensive, used almost exclusively in blends, contain twice the amount of caffeine, and are primarily used in making instant and commercial grade coffees.

The coffee-growing regions of the world lie between the Tropic of Cancer and the Tropic of Capricorn, as shown on the map on page 32. Coffees are often named after the ports from which they are exported, as well as their native countries or districts. However, understanding the geography that is the basis for these exotic names is not enough. Other modifiers attached to the name might denote altitude, method of processing, quality, size or shape of the bean. Flavors (chocolate, almond, etc.), roasts (Vienna, Espresso, French, etc.), blends (Mocha-Java, French Breakfast, etc.), even honorary titles (coffees named for celebrities) can be confusing without the help of your coffee merchant. Your local coffee merchant can help untangle the complexity of the coffees he sells.

If you understand that chocolate is an added flavor, or that Vienna is a degree of roast (see section on roasts) and not a coffee grown in Vienna, Austria, you are on the right track.

For your information, we have included a general listing of coffee-producing countries in the Appendix to acquaint you with the qualities of fine coffees.

DECAFFEINATION

Arabica coffee contains less caffeine than the lower grown robusta variety. Furthermore, the roasting process removes some caffeine, and the darker the roast, the less caffeine.

There are two methods of extracting caffeine from coffee. The traditional process involves the use of solvents (approved by the U.S. Food and Drug Administration) and high roasting temperatures. A newer method is a water-process. Both result in coffee that is approximately 98 percent caffeine-free. Specialty stores offer a wide assortment of coffees that are decaffeinated, allowing you to experience a variety of tastes, even if you prefer to avoid caffeine.

THE ROAST

It is the roasting of the green coffee beans that brings the oil to the surface of the bean, and hence unlocks the flavor. Roast designations, (i.e., Vienna, French, etc.), differ in meaning from region to region, so ask your specialty store for clarification.

In general, roasts are classified light, medium and dark. Since Americans have adopted the European preference for darker roasts, U.S. roasters have developed an assortment in varying shades to meet this growing consumer demand. As a result, a classic continental roast may look and taste differently when buying it in New York than that which is sold in San Francisco. So that you will be somewhat familiar with types of roasts, we have defined several that are used throughout the country. Please keep in mind, however, that darkness of roasts, even though it may have the same name, is not standardized and will vary.

Light Roast—The finished surface is light brown and dry. Also known as Cinnamon Roast in the northeast, but does not contain the spice. Results in a watery, bland tasting brew.

American Roast—Found in most commercial blends. Also known as City Roast. This roast is a light medium brown and has a dry surface. Labeled American Roast because of its historical preference by American coffee consumers.

Full City Roast—A medium roast that has been named for and traditionally preferred in New York City. Also favored in the deep south. Gives a deeper, heartier cup. Also known in some areas as High Roast.

Continental Roast—Also known as Vienna Roast, this medium, darker roast makes an excellent dessert coffee. It yields a rich, full-bodied, spicy cup.

Espresso Roast—On the west coast, this roast is lighter than in the east. Made especially for espresso machines, this roast is full-bodied, rich and smooth with a bite. The beans have an oily surface.

Italian Roast—The surface of the bean is dark brown and oily. An Italian Roast is favored by consumers in the coffee-producing countries. Depending on your area of the country, there may be little or no difference between this roast and espresso.

French Roast—Another dark roast that is delicious alone or used in blends. The taste is smooth, rich and like the other dark roasts, may have a burnt bottom note. A delightful roast for beans that have been decaffeinated.

Turkish Roast—This extremely dark, ebony-colored roast produces an almost charred flavor. Custom is to grind the beans to a powder consistency. To make, add 1 tablespoon of coffee to three ounces of water in an Ibrik. Add sugar and cardamom, boil and serve in a demitasse cup.

THE BLENDS

There is no limit to the possibilities for blending coffees. Different types of beans are blended to achieve consistency, favorable acidity and body, desired caffeine content, and personal taste preference. While many specialty coffee retailers offer a "private" blend, individual connoisseurs pride themselves on experimenting with combinations and discovering new tastes, then delighting their families and friends with their creations. It's easy and more economical than you might think since it takes only a few ounces of each kind of bean. Just remember to write down the proportions you use.

THE GRIND

The degree to which the coffee beans are ground depends upon the type of coffeemaker you use—and the grinder. Whatever your coffeemaker, use the grind of coffee recommended by the manufacturer. While retailers will grind your coffee beans for you, coffee that is ground loses flavor rapidly—even when stored in an air-tight container—so we recommend grinding your own as you use it.

THE BREW

The golden rule of good coffee: freshly ground coffee, water brought to a temperature of 195-200°, good method of brewing, and immediate consumption. Perhaps no one knows this process better than Mr. Coffee, Mr.

Coffee's automatic drip coffeemakers reach the ideal temperature for brewing to deliver a full-bodied, great-tasting cup of coffee. With an easy-to-use Mr. Coffee® coffeemaker and Mr. Coffee® paper filters you can't go wrong!

THE TASTE

The way your coffee tastes depends on a lot of very changeable components, as we have seen: the type of bean (arabica or robusta), the source of the beans (country and growing conditions), the roast of the beans (light, medium, or dark), the blend of the beans, and the method of brewing.

THE AROMA

One of the nicest aspects of coffee is aroma. Even non-coffee drinkers like the smell of coffee. Aroma is an indicator of freshness and should be considered when buying coffee. Good aroma usually means the coffee is fresh, and it should be captured in the cup.

Whether you buy flavored coffee beans, add spice to the grounds prior to brewing, create lush after-dinner treats, or use coffee to lend body and flavor to other foods, there's a world of excitement ahead of you.

BASIC COFFEE CONCENTRATE

Some of the recipes in this book call for Basic Coffee Concentrate. It is easy to make, and a convenient way to use coffee as a flavor enhancer.

Coffee concentrate is best brewed in an espresso machine, but if you don't have one, any coffee maker will do. Remember, however, good results depend to some extent on using at least two-thirds of the capacity of your coffee maker, which will undoubtedly yield a large amount of coffee concentrate. You can always share it with a friend, or you can freeze extra in ice cube trays, and enjoy it in iced coffee. The following proportion of coffee to water is recommended:

3   *coffee measures (6 tablespoons) dark roast coffee*
6   *ounces water*

Brew concentrate and allow to cool; freeze in ice cube trays.

Note: This concentrate is suggested for use only in flavoring foods.

BEVERAGES

JAMAICAN EGG NOG

1	quart prepared egg nog
1	cup brewed Jamaican coffee, cooled
1/2	cup rum or coffee liqueur
1	teaspoon vanilla
	nutmeg for garnish

Brew coffee and allow to cool. In a pitcher, combine egg nog, coffee, rum (or coffee liqueur), and vanilla. Pour mixture into individual punch cups, dust with nutmeg, and serve.

Yield: 8 servings

Café au Lait

    4   *coffee measures ground coffee*
    1   *cup (8 oz.) water*
   3/4   *cup milk*
         sugar to taste

Brew coffee. Heat milk, almost to a boil. Pour coffee and hot milk, preferably simultaneously, into large cups or mugs. Sweeten to taste. If you like the frothy finish that traditional steam infusers give to café au lait, whirl the hot milk in a blender (or use a whisk or hand mixer) before filling cups. Voila!

Yield: 3–4 servings

Coffee Ice Cream Soda

    2   *tablespoons coffee concentrate made with Viennese cinnamon coffee (or 2 cubes, if frozen, see page 9)*
         sweetener, as desired
    2   *tablespoons milk*
    2   *scoops coffee ice cream*
    6   *oz. carbonated water, chilled*
         whipped cream, cinnamon, and a whole coffee bean for garnish

Place (defrosted) coffee concentrate in tall glass and sweeten to taste. Add ice cream; fill with carbonated water. Garnish with whipped cream and a coffee bean. Serve with a straw and a long-handled spoon.

Yield: 1 serving

Chocolate Coffee Ice Cream Soda

    2   *tablespoons coffee concentrate made with Columbian or chocolate flavored coffee (or 2 cubes, if frozen, see page 9)*
    2   *tablespoons milk*
    2   *scoops coffee ice cream*
    6   *oz. carbonated chocolate soda, chilled*
         whipped cream and cherry, as garnish

Place (defrosted) coffee concentrate in tall glass. Add ice cream; fill with chocolate soda. Garnish with whipped cream and cherry. Serve with a straw and a long-handled spoon.

Yield: 1 serving.

Coffee Concentrate Café au Lait

6 ounces milk
2 cubes coffee concentrate (see page 9)
   sugar to taste

Heat milk almost to a boil. Add coffee concentrate cubes and stir until melted. Sweeten to taste; pour into mug.

Yield: 1 serving

Note: If desired, whip 3 tablespoons of the hot milk until frothy and "top off" each cup.

Irish Coffee

1 oz. Irish cream liqueur
1 teaspoon sugar (or to taste)
4 oz. freshly brewed hazelnut cream coffee
   whipped cream (sweetened, if desired)

In a heavy, stemmed glass, add liqueur, sugar, and a splash of the hot coffee. Stir till sugar dissolves. Add balance of coffee and gently lay whipped cream on top. Sip hot beverage through cold cream topping for a kaleidoscope of taste sensations.

Yield: 1 serving

Camper's Java

4   tablespoons fine ground Java coffee
1/4 teaspoon ground nutmeg
1/2 teaspoon butter extract
1/2 teaspoon rum extract

Place ground coffee, nutmeg, and extracts in a plastic zipper bag. Seal and shake well to blend.

To prepare, place coffee mixture in paper filter cone and pour 4 cups hot water through. (Don't forget to take along sweetener in a separate container.)

Yield: 4 servings

Café Caribe

4	tablespoons fine ground Jamaican coffee
1/2	teaspoon dried ground orange peel
1/4	teaspoon ground cinnamon
1	inch vanilla bean
	dash ground cloves

Place ingredients in plastic zipper bag. Seal and shake well. To brew, place coffee mixture in paper filter cone, and pour 4 cups hot water through.

Yield: 4 servings

Café Brûlot

1	cup brandy
3	tablespoons sugar
1	teaspoon grated orange peel
1/2	teaspoon grated lemon peel
6	whole cloves
4	whole allspice
1	cinnamon stick
1	teaspoon vanilla extract
3	cups double-strength coffee

Have ready a heat-proof serving bowl. Heat the brandy, sugar, orange and lemon peel, cloves, allspice, cinnamon stick and vanilla in a small saucepan over medium heat. Do not boil.

When brandy mixture is hot, pour into the heat-proof serving bowl. Darken the room, and carefully ignite brandy (for safety's sake, you might prefer to ignite a metal ladle of the brandy mixture and add this to the serving bowl). Let the brandy burn for 60 seconds. Slowly pour hot coffee into the flaming brandy. Stir mixture.

Yield: 6 servings

Easy Espresso and Cappuccino

4	coffee measures (1/2 cup) dark roast coffee
1 1/2	cups (12 oz.) water
4	twists of lemon peel
	sugar to taste

Brew coffee in your choice of coffeemaker. If you have an espresso pot or machine, follow manufacturer's suggested proportions of coffee and water. Pour coffee in demitasse cups, garnish with lemon twist, and offer sugar to guests.

Yield: 4 servings

Cappuccino variation:

Pour 2 parts brewed espresso and 1 part hot milk into tall mugs. Sprinkle with cinnamon and nutmeg, or grated chocolate.

Espresso de Menthe:

Measure 1–2 tablespoons Creme de Menthe into each demitasse cup; fill with espresso, leaving room for a dollop of whipped cream on top.

Caffè Latte

4	oz. brewed Italian roast espresso
4	oz. steamed milk
	sweetener as desired
	ice cubes (made from leftover flavored coffee, if desired)
	ground cinnamon for garnish, optional

Add (sweetened) hot espresso and steamed milk to a tall glass of ice. Stir. If desired, sprinkle top with ground cinnamon. Serve with a straw.

Yield: 1 serving

Hot Buttered Coffee

1	teaspoon unsalted butter
1	teaspoon brown sugar
5–6	ounces freshly brewed Jamaican coffee, steaming
1	whole clove
1	tablespoon dark rum
1/8	teaspoon grated nutmeg

Put butter in an Irish coffee glass or mug, then pour in the steaming coffee. Add brown sugar and stir until dissolved. Add clove and rum. Dust with nutmeg.

Yield: 1 serving

Italian Coffee

4	ounces freshly brewed Italian roast coffee
	Sweetener, as desired
1	tablespoon Amaretto
1	tablespoon brandy
1/4	cup heavy cream
1/4	teaspoon cinnamon

Pour coffee into a mug or an Irish coffee glass. Sweeten, if desired. Add the almond liqueur and brandy and stir. Pour the cream carefully over the back of a teaspoon so that it floats on top of the drink. Dust with cinnamon.

Yield: 1 serving

COFFEE ROYALE

4	ounces freshly brewed double-strength Kona coffee
	Sweetener, as desired
1	tablespoon Drambuie
1/4	teaspoon cardamom (optional)
1/4	cup heavy cream

Pour hot coffee into an Irish coffee glass. Add sweetener, if desired. Add Drambuie and stir. Add cardamom to cream and stir, then pour cream carefully over the back of a teaspoon so that it floats on top of the drink.

Yield: 1 serving

COFFEE FRAPPE

Ice cube tray of coffee concentrate (see page 9)
Favorite flavored double-strength coffee, brewed and cooled (i.e., Amaretto, Irish Cream, Vanilla Nut Cream, etc.)
Sweetener, as desired
Cream or milk (optional)

Crush coffee cubes and add to individual glasses. Sweeten the brewed coffee, if desired. Pour brewed coffee over cracked ice. Add cream and stir.

CHOCO-MOCHA SMOOTHIE

2	tablespoons chocolate syrup
1	tablespoon coffee concentrate made with Mocha Java coffee (or 1 cube, if frozen, see page 9)
1–2	scoops coffee ice cream
4–6 oz.	milk (white or chocolate)

Defrost coffee concentrate if necessary. Add all ingredients to blender container. Blend till smooth.

Yield: 1 serving

Entrees and More

Seafood Quiche

1	pastry pie crust (see page 37)
1/2	tablespoon coffee concentrate (see page 9)
1/2	cup cream
1 1/2	cups Swiss cheese
1 1/2	teaspoons flour
2	eggs, beaten
1/4	teaspoon freshly ground black pepper
1 1/2	cups shrimp, steamed and peeled or a combination of seafood
2	tablespoons capers

Prepare pie crust and set aside. Blend coffee into the cream. Combine cheese and flour. Add cream, eggs, pepper, shrimp, and capers. Pour mixture into pie crust and place in preheated 400° oven for 30 minutes or until golden and puffed. Allow to cool for 10 minutes before slicing.

Variation: For vegetarians, substitute 1 1/2 cups chopped vegetables in place of seafood. A combination of green and red peppers and onion, or spinach and cherry tomatoes is delicious. Be sure to steam or sauté lightly before adding to custard base.

Yield: 6 servings

CHICKEN TERIYAKI

8	pieces boneless chicken breast (or favorite chicken parts)
2/3	cup tamari or soy sauce
2	tablespoons fresh ginger root, grated
2	tablespoons honey
1/2	cup lemon juice
1/3	cup brewed coffee, cooled
1	small clove garlic, minced
2	teaspoons cornstarch
2	tablespoons cold water

Wash chicken and dry on paper towels. Place pieces in a large mixing bowl. Combine soy sauce, ginger, honey, lemon juice, coffee, and garlic in a large measuring cup, and mix together. Pour over chicken pieces. Cover bowl and place in refrigerator overnight or for at least 5 hours; turn chicken pieces occasionally to marinate evenly.

Preheat oven to 325°. Place chicken in a shallow ovenproof baking dish. Pour marinade over chicken. Bake, uncovered, on middle rack for 1 hour or until chicken is tender and juices run clear. Baste chicken with marinade once during baking. Remove chicken. Liquid in baking dish may be thickened before serving: mix cornstarch and water; slowly add to marinade in baking dish, stirring constantly until thickened. Pour over chicken and serve.

Yield: 6–8 servings

COFFEE GLAZED HAM

1	ham
3/4	cup dark brown sugar
1	teaspoon dry mustard
1	tablespoon orange (or any fruit) juice
4	teaspoons brewed coffee
	whole cloves

Bake ham at 350° for 30–60 minutes (depending upon size of ham). Mix remaining ingredients together, except for the cloves. Remove ham from oven and slash diagonally, first in one direction then across (forming diamonds). Stud intersecting cuts with whole cloves. Pour glaze over ham, and return to oven for another 30–60 minutes.

Yield: 8–10 servings

LASAGNA

2	cups Coffee Tomato Sauce (see below) or Tomato Chutney (see page 50)
1	pound lean ground beef, cooked until done
5	lasagna noodles, broken in half and cooked
10	ounces ricotta cheese
1/4	cup parmesan cheese, grated
12	ounces mozzarella cheese, sliced

Preheat oven to 375°. Combine tomato sauce and meat. Butter the bottom and sides of a 9"x13" baking pan. Put in 2 noodles as a first layer. Then put in a layer of meat/tomato sauce mixture, a layer of ricotta, a shake of Parmesan, and then some mozzarella. Start again with the noodles and keep doing this, ending with the mozzarella. Bake for 30 minutes.

Variation: Substitute 20-ounces of frozen spinach, cooked and drained, in place of beef. Be creative and use any favorite vegetable.

Yield: 6 servings

COFFEE TOMATO SAUCE

1	tablespoon oil
4	spring onions, minced
1–3	cloves garlic, minced
1/4	cup mushrooms, sliced
6	ounces tomato paste
3/4	cup strong, brewed coffee
3/4	cup beef or vegetable stock
1	teaspoon oregano
1	teaspoon basil
1/2	teaspoon paprika
1/4	teaspoon salt and pepper, or to taste

Pour oil into large pan and sauté onions, garlic, and mushrooms. Add tomato paste and blend. Stir in coffee and stock and season with oregano, basil, salt, and pepper. Cook until thickened.

Yield: approximately 2 cups

BEEF CURRY

1/2	cup vegetable oil
2	medium onions, sliced
1	tablespoon garlic, minced
1	tablespoon ginger, scraped and minced
1	tablespoon ground coriander
2	teaspoons curry powder
1/2	teaspoon paprika
1	cup tomatoes
1 1/2	pounds beef, cubed
2	cups brewed coffee
1	cup water
2	medium potatoes, peeled and sliced
	salt to taste
2	sprigs fresh parsley, chopped

In a heavy pan heat oil then sauté onions until they are light golden brown (about 12 minutes), stirring occasionally. Add garlic and ginger to pan and cook over medium heat, while stirring, until garlic is a light brown (approximately 4 minutes). Add coriander, curry powder and paprika and stir for 1 minute. Add tomatoes and cook for 4 minutes. Add meat and cook until meat is browned, stirring occasionally. Add coffee and water and bring to a boil. Reduce heat to medium and cook, covered tightly, 20 minutes. Add potatoes and stir. Cover tightly and simmer for another 40 minutes. Add salt if desired. Garnish with parsley; serve with rice.

Yield: 6 servings

INSTANT FLAVOR

Sprinkle ground cinnamon over grounds and brew as usual, or add ground cloves, cardamom, nutmeg, or almond extract similarly. After brewing, try dropping a candy lemon drop in your cup; stir until it melts.

CHOP SUEY WITH PORK

1/2	cup chopped onion
1	cup chopped celery
1/2	cup chopped green pepper
2	tablespoons oil
1/4	pound mushrooms, sliced
2	cups pork, cut in one-inch strips and cooked
1	cup brewed coffee
1	cup chicken stock
2	tablespoons tamari sauce or soy sauce
2	tablespoons cornstarch
1/4	cup cold water
1	cup fresh bean sprouts

In a wok, sauté onion, celery, and green pepper in oil until tender. Add mushrooms and sauté 2 more minutes. Add pork, coffee, stock, and tamari sauce, and simmer while stirring.

Dissolve cornstarch in cold water and gradually add to pork mixture, stirring until sauce is thickened. Add bean sprouts and serve over steamed rice or crunchy chow mein noodles.

Yield: 6 servings

PEPPERCORN CHICKEN

1	tablespoon cracked peppercorns (or more, to taste)
6	pieces boneless chicken breast
1	tablespoon oil
1	tablespoon brandy
2	tablespoons chopped chives or scallions
1/4	cup coffee concentrate (page 9)
3	tablespoons worcestershire sauce
2	tablespoons ketchup
2	tablespoons margarine
1	tablespoon freshly chopped parsley

Pound pepper into both sides of chicken pieces. Heat oil in skillet, and brown chicken evenly. Turn heat very low, cover, and cook about 10 minutes more or till done and juices run clear. Remove chicken from pan and keep warm. Turn heat to medium, add brandy and bring to a boil; add chives and coffee concentrate; lower heat and simmer 1 minute. Add worcestershire sauce and ketchup, stirring constantly. When hot and blended, quickly stir in margarine and parsley. Distribute sauce over chicken and serve.

Yield: 4–6 servings

Tandoori Chicken

1	chicken (about 2 1/2 pounds), skinned
3	tablespoons lemon juice
2	tablespoons coffee concentrate (see page 9)
1/8	teaspoon saffron threads
1	teaspoon hot water
1 1/2	teaspoons cumin seeds
3	teaspoons coriander seeds
4	tablespoons plain yogurt
1	tablespoon minced garlic
1	tablespoon fresh ginger, scraped and grated
3	tablespoons grated onion
1/2	teaspoon chili powder
1/2	teaspoon turmeric powder
1/2	teaspoon salt (optional)
2	tablespoons butter, melted
	thinly sliced tomato, for garnish

Start this typical Indian dish the day before you plan to serve it. Rinse chicken and allow to drain in a colander for at least 15 minutes. Pat dry and cut 6 slits, 2–3 inches long and 1/4 inch deep into the breasts, legs, and thighs. Rub lemon juice and coffee concentrate over the chicken and inside slits and set aside. After 10 minutes, turn chicken, baste with lemon juice, and set aside for another 10 minutes. Baste again with lemon juice.

Soak the saffron threads in the water until dissolved. Heat a pan and stir in cumin seeds and coriander seeds and roast for 1 minute over moderately high heat. Remove immediately and grind to a powder in a blender. Place yogurt into a small bowl. Blend in the saffron, ground spices, garlic, ginger, onion, chili powder, turmeric powder, and salt.

Pour excess lemon juice off chicken. Place chicken on its back in a baking dish, spread the blended yogurt mixture over it and inside the slits as well. Cover securely and set aside for 18 hours in refrigerator. To cook, baste with marinade and bake at 350° for 45 minutes, or until done, turning chicken over half-way through cooking. Reset oven to broil, carefully roll chicken over on its back, brush on butter and broil 5 minutes for a nice golden finish. Place on a serving platter and garnish with tomato slices.

Yield: 4 servings

CRÊPES DIVAN

CRÊPES:

4	eggs
1/4	cup brewed coffee
1 1/2	cups milk
1 1/2	cups flour
1	tablespoon butter or margarine, melted
1/2	teaspoon salt
1/4	teaspoon baking powder

Beat eggs slightly. Stir coffee into milk and pour into the eggs. Stir in flour. Beat until smooth. Add butter, salt and baking powder. Beat smooth. Let stand 5 minutes.

Brush a 6-inch skillet lightly with a little butter. When pan is hot, add 3–4 tablespoons batter to skillet, tipping skillet quickly so batter will run around pan thinly and completely cover the bottom of pan. Turn heat down and let cook through; they need not be turned, but bottom should be golden. If crêpes are too thick, use less batter. Stack crêpes, cover with a towel and keep warm in a slow oven.

Tip: If you have crêpes left over, wrap them carefully with a square of waxed paper between each one, then completely in foil, and freeze them.

Yield: 20 crêpes

FILLING:

2	(10 ounce) packages frozen chopped broccoli
2	tablespoons butter or margarine
2	tablespoons chopped onion
1	can (6 ounces) chopped mushrooms, drained
2	tablespoons flour
1/2	cup light cream
1/2	cup chicken broth (may use bouillon cube)
2	tablespoons grated Parmesan Cheese
2	cans (5 ounces) boneless, chunked chicken
1	teaspoon salt (optional)
1/8	teaspoon pepper

Cook broccoli according to package directions. Do not overcook. Drain well. In a saucepan, melt butter and sauté onion and mushrooms until lightly browned. Stir in flour. Add cream and chicken broth slowly and cook, stirring until thickened. Mix in remaining ingredients, including the broccoli and chicken. The mixture will be quite thick. Add salt and pepper.

(continued on next page)

SAUCE:

1/4	cup butter or margarine
1/4	cup flour
1 3/4	cups light cream
2	cups milk
1 1/2	cups grated Parmesan cheese
2	teaspoons Dijon mustard
1	teaspoon salt
	paprika

Melt butter and stir in flour. Add cream and milk. Cook and stir until smooth and thickened. Add cheese, mustard and salt and cook gently until smooth and cheese has melted completely.

To assemble the crêpes, spread each with filling, roll up and place seam-side down in 2 greased shallow casseroles. Pour sauce over all, sprinkle with paprika, and bake in a moderate oven, 350°, 25–30 minutes, until bubbly and slightly browned.

Note: The crêpes may be made a day before, kept covered and refrigerated. Or make them a week in advance and freeze them. The sauce and the filling may be prepared the night before or the morning of the luncheon. Assemble crêpes for baking (without sauce) about an hour before guests arrive. Thirty minutes before serving, heat sauce, pour over crêpes and bake.

Yield: 8 servings, 2 crêpes each

CUTTING DOWN ON CAFFEINE?

When buying coffee beans, combine caffeinated and decaffeinated varieties. Shake bag for even distribution.

The result: a "half-caff" brew.

PEPPER STEAK

2	cups sliced green pepper, cut into $1/2$-inch-wide strips
$1/4$	cup oil
$1/2$	cup coarsely chopped onion
1	tablespoon fresh ginger, grated
$1 1/2$	pounds sirloin steak, cut in strips 1" thick by 3" long
2	tablespoons cornstarch
$1/4$	cup tamari or soy sauce
3	tablespoons dry sherry
$1/2$	cup brewed coffee

Stir-fry green peppers in 2 tablespoons of the oil for one minute. Cover skillet and simmer another minute, then remove cover and stir again. Add onion and ginger. Sauté until transparent. Move vegetables to one side. Add strips of sirloin and additional oil as needed, one tablespoon at a time. Stir-fry until no pink shows, then toss with vegetables.

Combine cornstarch, tamari sauce, and sherry and blend thoroughly while slowly adding coffee. Pour mixture over sirloin and vegetables, stirring constantly. Cook over medium heat for 2 minutes. Remove from heat and serve immediately over steamed rice.

Yield: 4 servings

Souvlaki (Greek Sandwich)

1/2	cup olive or vegetable oil
1/4	cup red wine vinegar
1/4	cup lemon juice
1/4	cup brewed coffee
1	teaspoon dried oregano
3	cloves garlic, pressed
1	teaspoon cayenne pepper
1	teaspoon Dijon mustard
1/2	teaspoon freshly ground black pepper
	pinch of salt, or to taste
2 1/2	pounds lamb or beef, cut into 2-inch slices
1	pint cherry tomatoes
1	medium onion
	pita bread
	feta cheese, crumbled

Mix oil, vinegar, lemon juice, coffee, oregano, garlic, cayenne, mustard, pepper and salt. Add lamb or beef, and marinate for at least 2 hours (or overnight in refrigerator), stirring occasionally. Cut tomatoes in half and slice onion and set aside. Place meat on a charcoal grill or under a broiler and grill until done. If using large-size pita, cut each piece in half; for small pita, slit open just enough to fill. Warm the pita and stuff with the meat; add tomato and onion, and feta cheese. If desired, spoon dressing on top.

Dressing:

1/2	cup chopped cucumber
1/2	cup sour cream
1/2	cup plain yogurt
1–2	teaspoons minced fresh garlic

Peel cucumber and chop fine, place in double thickness of paper towel and squeeze out as much liquid as possible. Set aside. Combine sour cream, yogurt and garlic. Squeeze cucumber again, then add to sour cream mixture. Mix. Use to top Souvlaki or as a dip for pita bread.

Yield: 8–10 servings

MINTY LAMB STEW

2	pounds lean lamb or beef, in chunks
3	tablespoons butter
5	cups water
1	cup brewed coffee
2	tablespoons fresh, chopped parsley
1	tablespoon fresh, chopped mint
1/8	teaspoon sage
1/8	teaspoon paprika
1/8	teaspoon cayenne pepper
1/8	teaspoon ground cloves
1/8	teaspoon onion powder
2	medium potatoes, peeled and cut in chunks
2	large carrots, cut in 1 1/2 inch pieces
2	onions, cut in fourths
1	large bell pepper, cut into strips
3	ounces tomato paste
3–4	tablespoons flour
1/4	cup cold water
	salt and pepper to taste
	fresh mint sprigs

Brown meat in butter in large pot. Add water and coffee and bring to a boil, then reduce heat, add spices and simmer for 1 1/2 hours, covered. Add potatoes, carrots, onions, and bell pepper and bring to a boil. Then simmer, covered for an additional 35 minutes, or until vegetables are tender.

Stir in tomato paste. Dissolve flour in 1/4 cup water, blend well. Pour into pot with meat and vegetables and stir until smooth. Cook an additional 10 minutes, covered. Add salt and pepper. Garnish with mint sprigs before serving.

Yield: 6 servings

COFFEE CLEAN-UP

Cups which have been stained by coffee should be rinsed with vinegar and then rubbed with a cloth dipped in salt. Wash in soapy water afterwards, then rinse and dry. Try sea salt or urn cleaner, too.

Veal Paprika

6	veal cutlets, approximately 2 pounds
1	cup lemon juice
1/2	teaspoon salt
1	cup flour
1	cup onions, chopped
	oil for sautéing
1 1/2	tablespoons paprika
1/2	cup strong, brewed coffee
2	tablespoons cornstarch
1	cup plain yogurt
	paprika and chopped fresh basil, for garnish

Marinate veal cutlets in lemon juice for an hour (turn them after the first 30 minutes). Pat cutlets dry then combine salt and flour. Dip cutlets in flour mixture and shake off excess.

Sauté onions in oil until translucent. Add cutlets and more oil and fry until lightly brown on both sides. Stir in paprika, then add coffee and bring to a boil, stirring.

Place cutlets in baking dish, pour onion-coffee mixture over cutlets, cover and bake in preheated 350° oven until tender, about 1 hour.

Stir cornstarch into yogurt and place in a skillet. Pour the liquid off the baked cutlets into the yogurt mixture, stirring. Simmer for 5 minutes, or until sauce is thickened. Pour sauce over cutlets and garnish. Serve with noodles or rice.

Yield: 4 servings

Moving?

Tie ground coffee in cheese cloth pouches and place in freezer and refrigerator to keep the interior fresh and clean-smelling and retard mildew.

Moussaka

      about 1/2 cup olive oil
1   large or 2 small eggplants, sliced thinly
1   cup chopped green pepper
3/4   cup chopped onion
1   clove garlic, minced
1   pound ground lamb or ground beef
1/2   cup Amaretto coffee
2   cups fresh tomatoes, peeled and chopped
1   cup tomato puree
1/2   teaspoon basil
1/2   teaspoon thyme
1   teaspoon salt
1/4   teaspoon freshly ground black pepper
1/4   cup fine bread crumbs
1/2   cup Parmesan cheese

Bechamel Sauce:
2   tablespoons butter
2   tablespoons flour
1 1/2 cups milk
1   teaspoon lemon juice
      a grating of nutmeg
      salt and white pepper to taste.

Preheat oven to 375°. Lightly oil a two-quart casserole; set aside. Put two tablespoons oil in a large skillet, and place over medium heat. Add eggplant slices, a few at a time, and brown quickly on both sides. Add more oil to skillet as needed. Add one tablespoon of the oil to the same skillet. Sauté green pepper and onion over low heat until tender, about 5 minutes. Add garlic and meat and cook over medium heat, until lightly browned. Pour excess fat from meat and vegetable mixture.

Return skillet to low heat; add coffee, tomatoes, tomato puree, basil, thyme, salt, and pepper. Simmer mixture for 10 to 15 minutes, uncovered. Remove from heat. Combine bread crumbs and Parmesan cheese. Beginning and ending with meat sauce, arrange alternate layers of meat sauce and eggplant slices in prepared casserole. Sprinkle Parmesan mixture over each layer of meat sauce, except bottom. Set aside.

Bechamel Sauce: In a saucepan, melt butter over low heat; add flour and stir until blended. Gradually add milk; stir over low heat for 3 to 5 minutes, until sauce thickens. Add lemon juice, nutmeg, salt and pepper. Pour Bechamel sauce over moussaka casserole. Bake on middle rack, uncovered, for 40 minutes or until eggplant is tender. Remove moussaka from oven and let stand for 10 minutes before serving.

Yield: 6 large servings

Tomato Chutney

5	tablespoons mustard oil, or vegetable oil
1/4	teaspoon fenugreek seeds
1 1/2	cups onions, chopped
1 1/2	tablespoons minced garlic
2	tablespoons minced ginger
8	large tomatoes, cut into 1" cubes
1/4	cup strong, brewed coffee
3–5	small green chilis
1	teaspoon turmeric powder
1 1/2	teaspoons paprika
1	tablespoon arrowroot, optional

In a 4-quart heavy-bottomed pot, heat oil until it is almost smoking. Drop in fenugreek seeds and when they are almost black, add onions and fry over medium heat until golden brown (about 10 minutes). Add 1 tablespoon of garlic and 1 teaspoon of ginger and fry over moderately high heat for 2 minutes.

Add tomatoes, coffee, 1/2 tablespoon garlic, 1 1/2 tablespoons ginger, chilis, turmeric powder, and paprika and bring to a boil. Lower heat to moderate, cover, and cook 15 minutes. Stir occasionally. Uncover and cook over moderately high heat until liquid thickens and resembles a thick sauce (about 1 1/2 hours). If a thickening agent is necessary, stir 1/8 cup of liquid from chutney into the arrowroot. When blended, add arrowroot mixture to the rest of the chutney. Stir frequently during last stages of cooking.

Yield: 6 servings

Tip: this dish is a delicious addition to most meals. It freezes well and can be reheated many weeks later with no loss of flavor.

Mexican Dip

1	cup nacho cheese (chilis & cheese)
1	cup canned chili with beans
1/4	cup brewed coffee

Heat cheese over low heat; add chili and coffee, mix well. Serve with corn chips or raw turnip slices.

Yield: 4 servings

Tomato Aspic

2 1/2   teaspoons unflavored gelatin
1/4   cup cold water
1/3   cup boiling water
1/2   cup tomato juice
1/4   cup catsup
1   tablespoon lemon juice
1 1/2   teaspoons coffee concentrate (see page 9)
2   tablespoons chopped green pepper
2   tablespoons chopped onion or scallion
2   tablespoons celery
   Mayonnaise

Put the cold water in a 1 quart bowl and sprinkle the gelatin over it. Let stand for 5 minutes to soften. Add boiling water and stir until gelatin is completely dissolved. Stir in tomato juice, catsup, lemon juice, coffee concentrate, green pepper, onion and celery. Taste and add salt if needed. Pour into mold or dish and chill in the refrigerator until set. Garnish with mayonnaise.

Yield: 3–4 servings

Maple Walnut Baked Beans

1   pound dried baby lima beans
1/2   cup butter or margarine
5   tablespoons tomato ketchup
3/4   cup dark brown sugar
1   teaspoon dry mustard
1/4   cup brewed maple walnut flavored coffee
1/4   cup bean stock

Soak beans in water to cover, overnight. Add more water if necessary to cover beans by 1 inch and bring to a boil. Reduce heat and simmer 1 hour. Drain, reserving stock. Place beans in heavy casserole with lid. Add remaining ingredients and stir gently until mixed. Bake at 350° covered for 3 hours, checking every 30–45 minutes, and adding more bean stock as needed to keep from drying out.

Almost all of the world's coffe
Cancer and the T

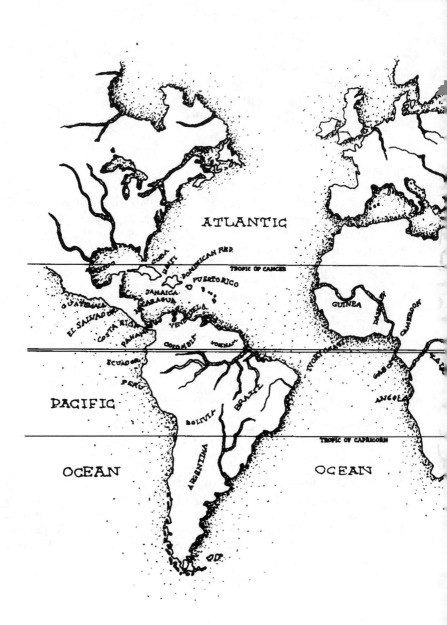

grown between the Tropic of
c of Capricorn.

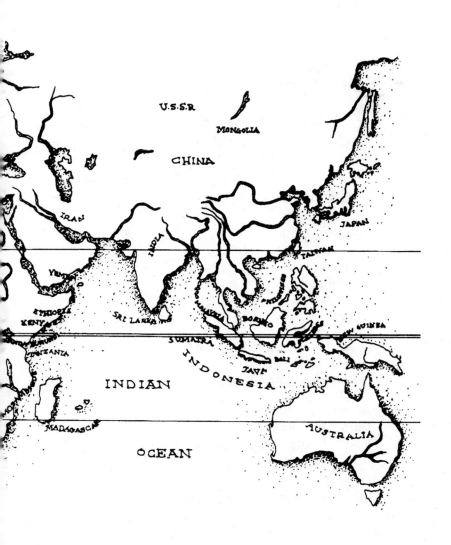

DESSERTS

APRICOT BROWNIES

2	cups strong coffee
1 1/2	cups sugar, divided
2	tablespoons cocoa
3/4	cup chopped, dried apricots
1/3	cup butter
1/2	teaspoon vanilla
2	eggs
1 1/2	cups whole wheat flour, sifted
1/2	teaspoon baking soda
2	teaspoons baking powder
1/2	teaspoon cinnamon
1/2	teaspoon nutmeg
1/2	teaspoon ground cloves
	9"x13" baking pan, greased and floured
	powdered sugar

Combine coffee, 1/2 cup sugar, and cocoa in a sauce pan; add apricots. Bring to a boil, reduce heat and simmer for 10–15 minutes. Cool. Beat the butter, adding remaining sugar a little at a time; beat well. Add vanilla and eggs (one at a time), beating constantly. Sift dry ingredients together and blend into the butter mixture alternately with the cooled coffee mixture; stir until well blended. Pour batter into prepared pan and bake at 350° for 40–55 minutes or until done. Cool; sprinkle with powdered sugar, and cut into squares.

Yield: about 3 dozen brownies

CHOCOLATE COFFEE PIE

CRUST:

1/2	cup butter
1	cup all-purpose flour
1	cup finely chopped walnuts

FILLING:

1	8-ounce package cream cheese, softened
1	cup confectioners' sugar, sifted
14	ounces frozen whipped dessert topping, thawed
2	(3 1/2–4 ounce) packages instant chocolate pudding
2 3/4	cups milk
1/4	cup coffee concentrate (see page 9)
	grated chocolate for garnish

In mixing bowl, cut butter into flour until crumbly. Stir in 3/4 cup of the walnuts. Press mixture evenly over bottom of a 13x9x2 inch baking dish. Bake at 350° for 20 minutes. Cool. Meanwhile, in a small bowl, beat cream cheese on low speed until fluffy; beat in confectioners' sugar and half of the thawed whipped topping. Spread over crust. Chill.

In a large bowl, combine pudding mix, milk, and coffee concentrate, then beat with rotary beater for two minutes. Spoon over the chilled cream cheese layer. Chill until firm, several hours or overnight. Top with remaining thawed whipped topping. Sprinkle with remaining chopped nuts and grated chocolate.

Yield: 8 servings

COFFEE CHIFFON CAKE

5	*eggs, separated, at room temperature*
1/2	*teaspoon cream of tartar*
1 1/4	*cups sugar*
2	*cups cake flour*
1	*cup chopped pecans*
1	*tablespoon baking powder*
1/2	*teaspoon salt*
3/4	*cup strong coffee, cold*
1/4	*cup vegetable oil*
1	*teaspoon vanilla extract*
1	*teaspoon almond extract*

ICING:

2 1/2	*cups confectioners' sugar*
1	*teaspoon vanilla*
1/4	*cup café au lait, cold*
	whole pecans and coffee beans

Preheat oven to 350°. In a medium bowl beat egg whites and cream of tartar at high speed until stiff peaks form. Set aside. In another bowl mix sugar, flour, pecans, baking powder and salt. Reserve. Combine coffee, egg yolks, oil, vanilla and almond extracts, and blend. Add dry ingredients and mix well. Carefully fold in egg whites, pour into ungreased tube or Bundt pan, and bake for 50 minutes to an hour, or until top springs back when lightly touched. Cool in pan for 5 minutes. Turn out onto serving plate and cool completely.

Variation: Substitute walnuts for pecans and walnut extract for vanilla and almond extracts.

To make icing, combine sugar and vanilla, gradually add café au lait. Mix until you reach a desired consistency to pour on cake. Reserve some frosting, add more confectioners' sugar to thicken it, and pipe around base of cake. Garnish with pecans (or walnuts) and coffee beans.

Yield: 10–12 servings

COFFEE PARFAITS

4 cups very strong coffee
4 teaspoons honey
2 tablespoons Amaretto (or 1 teaspoon almond extract)
1 pint coffee ice cream
1 pint vanilla ice cream
    grated semisweet chocolate
    slivered almonds

Mix coffee, honey, and Amaretto (or almond extract) and put into refrigerator trays. Freeze until crystals begin to form. Put into bowl and beat at high speed. Return to trays until frozen. Layer parfait glasses in the following order: one (small) scoop coffee ice cream, one scoop Amaretto mixture, one scoop vanilla ice cream, grated chocolate, and almonds. Repeat. Freeze, or serve immediately.

Variation: Substitute your favorite ice cream combinations and/or drizzle Fudge Sauce instead of grated chocolate.

Yield: 6–8 servings

MOCHA ICE CREAM

2 cups café au lait
2 tablespoons arrowroot
2 squares unsweetened chocolate
3/4 cup sugar
5 egg yolks, slightly beaten
2 cups heavy cream

In a double boiler, bring café au lait to a simmer. Take out 1 tablespoon of the café au lait, blend with arrowroot, then add to double boiler and cook over low heat, while stirring, until mixture thickens. Add chocolate squares and heat until melted. Combine sugar and egg yolks in another pan. Add café au lait mixture gradually, stirring constantly, and place pan over heat until mixture coats spoon (about 5 minutes). Cool for 10 minutes in freezer, then stir in heavy cream. Freeze in covered bowl until ice cream sets. For best results, beat ice cream until creamy once during freezing time.

Yield: 4–6 servings

VIENNESE CINNAMON DATE NUT BREAD

1 1/2	cups flour
1/2	cup wheat germ
1/2	cup walnuts, chopped
1	teaspoon baking powder
1	cup milk
1/2	cup strong Viennese Cinnamon coffee, cold
2	eggs, beaten
1/2	cup butter, melted
1/4	cup sugar
1/2	cup dates, chopped

Combine flour, wheat germ, walnuts, and baking powder in a large bowl. In another bowl pour the milk and coffee; add eggs, butter, sugar and dates. Gradually add the wet ingredients to the dry, mixing quickly. Pour into greased loaf pan and bake at 375° for 45–55 minutes, or until done.

Variation: Substitute fresh chopped cranberries for the dates and orange juice for the milk, increase sugar to 1/2 cup.

Yield: 1 loaf

FESTIVE COCONUT BALLS

This recipe should be made in a food processor with the steel blade.

1	cup shredded wheat cereal
1 1/2	cups quick oats
1 1/4	cups shredded sweetened coconut
1/2	teaspoon cinnamon
2	tablespoons coffee liqueur
1/3	cup honey
1/4	cup safflower oil (or any light oil)

Place shredded wheat in processor and blend. Add oats, 1 cup of the coconut and cinnamon and blend again. While food processor is on, add coffee liqueur, and drizzle in honey and oil. Roll mixture into bite-sized balls, then roll balls into remaining coconut. Refrigerate for at least an hour before serving.

Yield: About 2 dozen

FRUIT CREME/SHERBET

    2   *cups mango, chopped fine*, then frozen*
    1   *tablespoon coffee concentrate (see page 9)*
    1   *tablespoon cream (optional)*
  1/4   *cup sugar, or to taste*
         slivered pistachio nuts

Place frozen fruit into food processor (or blender, if you want sherbet) with the double blade. Turn on the processor. Add a teaspoon of the coffee concentrate at a time, until the ice cream is smooth. (If desired, add a little cream for a smoother consistency.) Add sugar and blend. Freeze. Serve in chilled dessert glasses, garnish with pistachios (or any nuts). Makes about 1 pint. (Note: If desired, spoon into serving dishes and freeze until needed. Remove from freezer 10–15 minutes before serving.)

Variations: Use any fruit or fruits in season. Good combinations are Raspberry/Papaya, Banana/Cherry, Peach/Blueberry, etc. Add 1/4 cup of nuts, chocolate chips, or coconut, if you like. Serving alternative: Cut oranges, lemons, or limes in half, scoop out pulp (reserve for another recipe or squeeze juice for a punch), then spoon Fruit Creme into rind shells and freeze for a spectacular presentation!

*The smaller the chopped frozen fruit, the easier it is to blend into a smooth ice cream. Also, the consistency may vary, depending upon the fruit you use.

Yield: 4 servings

CHOCOLATE PEANUT BUTTER FONDUE

    6   *oz. semisweet chocolate (or milk chocolate) morsels*
    4   *tablespoons heavy cream*
    1   *tablespoon coffee liqueur*
  1/4   *cup peanut butter*
  1/2   *teaspoon vanilla extract*
         strawberries, bananas, pineapple, kiwi, biscotti, and pound cake squares for dipping

In a ceramic fondue pot, place chocolate morsels, cream, liqueur, peanut butter, and vanilla. Over low heat, stir till melted and combined. Prepare a platter of fruit and cake for dipping. Give each guest a fondue fork and small plate.

Yield: 4 servings

KAHLUA CREAM

1 1/2	cups heavy cream
1	tablespoon unflavored gelatin
1	cup sour cream
1/4	cup Kahlua Liqueur
1/4	cup sugar
1/8	teaspoon cardamom, optional

Heat 1 1/2 cups heavy cream over low heat, then add gelatin and stir to dissolve. Add sour cream, Kahlua, sugar and cardamom, and blend until sugar has dissolved. Pour into mold and refrigerate. After gelatin sets, unmold, and garnish as follows:

TOPPING:

1/2	cup heavy cream, whipped
1	tablespoon Kahlua
	sprinkle of nutmeg

Whip cream; blend in Kahlua. Mound on top of gelatin and sprinkle with nutmeg.

Yield: 4 servings

PASTRY CRUST

1 1/2	cups sifted flour
1	tablespoon sugar
1/4	cup butter, very cold
3	tablespoons half-and-half, or sour cream
3	tablespoons coffee concentrate

Place flour and sugar in food processor, add pieces of butter, blending until mixture is crumbly. Combine half-and-half with coffee, and add to flour a little at a time, until the dough forms a ball. Chill dough for 1 hour. Roll out to fit a 9" pie pan. Use excess dough for lattice strips. Fill, adjust top, and bake, or prick empty shell with fork and bake at 350° for 8 to 10 minutes, or until golden brown. Fill when cool.

Yield: 1 crust

TIRAMISU

2	*3-ounce packages ladyfingers*
1/3	*cup brewed Italian roast coffee, espresso strength*
2	*tablespoons coffee liqueur*
2	*8-ounce packages cream cheese*
1/4	*cup milk*
3/4	*cup confectioner's sugar*
1	*teaspoon vanilla*
1	*cup whipping cream*
2	*teaspoons unsweetened cocoa powder*
	chocolate shavings, optional

Spread ladyfingers on a sheet of waxed paper; combine espresso and 1 tablespoon of the liqueur and drizzle over ladyfingers. Set aside. In a large bowl beat cream cheese and milk. Add the remining tablespoon of coffee liqueur; the confectioners' sugar, and vanilla; mix well.

Whip cream to stiff peaks and fold into cream cheese mixture. Line bottom of a souffle or trifle dish with half of the ladyfingers. Cover with half of the cheese mixture and sprinkle 1 teaspoon of the cocoa powder on top. Repeat layers. Chill at least 4 hours or overnight; garnish with chocolate shavings, if desired. (For a single-tier version, make one layer of Tiramisu in a 13x9x2 inch pan.)

Yield: 8–10 servings

BAKLAVA

8	sheets fillo pastry (12"x16")
1/2	cup butter, melted
1 1/4	cups very finely chopped walnuts
1/3	cup honey
1	teaspoon coffee liqueur
1/2	teaspoon ground cinnamon
1/2	cup honey
1	teaspoon lemon juice
1/2	teaspoon grated orange peel
1/2	teaspoon ground cloves

Preheat oven to 350°. Butter a 10x7 inch metal baking pan. Cut the 8 sheets of fillo pastry in half to make 16 half-sheets.

Brush 8 of the pastry sheets with butter and layer them into the pan.

Combine walnuts, 1/3 cup of the honey, coffee liqueur, and cinnamon. Spread the walnut mixture over fillo sheets in pan. Brush remaining 8 sheets of fillo with butter, and place on top of walnut mixture in pan.

Using a very sharp knife, cut pan of pastry diagonally to form diamond-shaped pieces. Brush remaining butter on top, and bake for 30 minutes, or until top is golden brown and crisp.

While Baklava is baking, combine the remaining 1/2 cup honey, lemon juice, orange peel, and cloves in a small saucepan. Heat to boiling, then lower heat and simmer the syrup mixture for 8 to 10 minutes. Remove Baklava from oven and immediately top with hot syrup mixture. Cool.

Yield: 12 servings

COFFEE CUBES

Use left over brewed coffee and pour into ice cube tray and freeze. Cubes can be added to iced coffee and won't dilute the flavor.

BISCOTTI

3	eggs
3/4	cup sugar
3/4	cup oil
1/4	teaspoon salt
1/2	teaspoon baking powder
1	tablespoon coffee liqueur
3/4	teaspoon almond extract
3/4	cup sliced almonds
2 1/2	cups flour
1/2	cup cornmeal
2	tablespoons cinnamon
1/2	cup sugar
1	tablespoon unsweetened cocoa powder

In a large mixing bowl, beat eggs. Add sugar and mix to combine. Add oil, salt, baking powder, coffee liqueur, almond extract, and almonds. Mix well. Add flour and cornmeal; combine. Set aside for five minutes.

Divide dough in half. On a cookie sheet, shape half the dough into a loaf 1 inch high and 2 inches wide. Add the cocoa to remaining half of dough in bowl and mix well. Shape like first loaf on cookie sheet.

Combine cinnamon and sugar and sprinkle on loaves. Bake at 350° for 30 minutes. Remove from oven, cut loaves across into 1-inch slices. Turn cut sides down and bake 15 minutes; turn to other side and bake 15 minutes more, or until toasted. Cool completely before storing.

Yield: 2 1/2 dozen

Fudge Sauce

2   squares semi-sweet chocolate
³/₄   cup café au lait (see page 12)
1   cup miniature marshmallows
1   teaspoon vanilla

Melt chocolate over low heat. Add café au lait and stir until well blended. Add marshmallows and continue stirring until they dissolve; add vanilla, and serve.

Variation: Add ¼ cup peanut butter (plain or chunky).

Yield: about 1 ½ cups

Coffee Lemon Bars

2 ¼   cups sifted all-purpose flour, divided
³/₄   cup sifted confectioners' sugar, divided
¼   cup plus 2 teaspoons coffee liqueur
2   sticks (1 cup) butter
4   eggs, beaten
2   cups granulated sugar
¼   cup freshly squeezed lemon juice
½   teaspoon baking powder

Sift together 2 cups of the flour and ½ cup of the confectioners' sugar. Add 2 teaspoons of the coffee liqueur. Cut in butter with pastry blender until mixture clings together. Press into a 13x9x2 inch baking pan. Bake at 350° for 20 to 25 minutes (or until barely turning tan).

Blend together the eggs, granulated sugar, the remaining ¼ cup coffee liqueur, and fresh lemon juice.

Sift together the remaining ¼ cup flour and the baking powder. Stir flour mixture into egg mixture. Pour over baked crust. Bake at 350° for 25 minutes, or until custard tests done.

Sprinkle with remaining confectioners' sugar. Cool. Cut into squares or bars.

Yield: About 30 pieces

Pecan Praline Bread Pudding

1 1/4	cups brown sugar
1/2	cup coarsely chopped pecans
1 1/2	tablespoons butter or margarine
4	slices raisin bread
3	eggs
1 3/4	cups milk
	dash salt
1 1/2	tablespoons coffee liqueur
	cinnamon

Place sugar in top of a double boiler; top with pecans. Butter each slice of bread; cut bread in squares and distribute on top of brown sugar.

Beat eggs; add milk, salt, and liqueur to eggs. Mix well, then pour over sugar and bread. Sprinkle with cinnamon. Do not stir.

Cover and place over simmering water for 60 minutes or till set. A sauce will form under the pudding. Serve in individual bowls and spoon sauce on top.

Optional Garnishes:

Half and Half
Whipped cream
Ice cream
Frozen yogurt

Yield: 6–8 servings

COFFEE COCONUT MOUSSE PIE

1	recipe Cashew Coconut Crust (page 47)
1	cup brewed Amaretto coffee, cooled
1	envelope unflavored gelatin
1/2	cup sugar
1/2	teaspoon vanilla extract
1	cup heavy cream
	shredded chocolate, optional

Preheat oven to 350°. Prepare Cashew Coconut Crust as directed on page 47. Cool completely.

Pour coffee into a small saucepan, then sprinkle gelatin on top. Let stand for a few minutes to soften. Stir mixture over very low heat until gelatin dissolves. Blend in sugar. Remove from heat, then stir in vanilla. Chill until mixture is syrupy, about 1 hour.

In a large bowl, whip cream until soft peaks form. Whisk in cold gelatin mixture. Spoon into crust. Sprinkle top with shredded chocolate. Chill until firm, at least 3 hours.

Yield: 6 servings

MINT MOCHA RASPBERRY BOMBE

1	pint coffee ice cream
1	pint raspberries
1	pint chocolate mint ice cream
1/2	pint raspberry sherbet
	Kirsch (or Framberry) liqueur
1	teaspoon coffee concentrate (see page 9)

Chill a 1 1/2 quart round mold. Allow the ice creams to soften slightly. When mold is very cold, line it with a one-inch layer of coffee ice cream. Sprinkle one-fourth of the raspberries over ice cream. Add a layer of chocolate mint ice cream, and finish with raspberry sherbet. Cover and place in freezer for several hours. Marinate the rest of the raspberries in liqueur and coffee concentrate. When ready to serve, dip mold quickly into very hot water. Dry it off and invert it on a serving dish. Top with marinated raspberries and serve in wedges. (Note: Heat a knife in hot water for easy slicing.)

Yield: 6 servings

Kiwi Lime Pie

1	Cashew Coconut Pie Crust, baked (below)
1	can (14 ounces) sweetened condensed milk
2	tablespoons coffee liqueur
2	eggs
2	teaspoons grated lime rind
1	tablespoon lime juice
1/4	teaspoon salt
2	large kiwi, peeled and sliced
	sweetened whipped cream, optional

Prepare pie crust, reserving 2 tablespoons of the crumb mixture.

Combine condensed milk, coffee liqueur, eggs, lime rind, lime juice, and salt. Arrange the slices of kiwi on bottom of pie shell. Pour filling into pie shell; sprinkle remaining crumb mixture on top.

Bake at 425° for 10 minutes; reduce temperature to 350°, and bake 50–60 minutes more or until knife inserted in center comes out clean.

Cool completely and refrigerate. If desired, top each serving with a dollop of sweetened whipped cream.

Yield: 6–8 servings

Cashew Coconut Crust

1/2	cup raw cashews, ground
1/2	cup sweetened shredded coconut
1/2	cup wheat germ
3–4	tablespoons butter, melted

Combine ingredients and press into 9" pie pan. Place crust in preheated 350° oven for 5 minutes. Cool, then pour in filling of your choice.

Yield: One 9" crust

DID YOU KNOW?

Since the Boston Tea Party, coffee has been America's drink, and we consume more than half the world's coffee production!

Strawberry Coffee Cheesecake

1	Graham Cracker Crust, below
1	8-ounce package cream cheese, softened
2	eggs, separated
2/3	cup sugar
2	tablespoons coffee liqueur
1/2	teaspoon grated lemon rind
1	pint fresh strawberries

Prepare pie crust; bake and cool. Whip cream cheese until light; add egg yolks, sugar, coffee liqueur, and lemon rind. Mix well. Beat egg whites until stiff and fold into cream cheese mixture. Place half of the strawberries on bottom of prepared pie crust. Pour cream cheese mixture on top. Bake at 350° for 25–30 minutes; allow to cool completely. Garnish with remaining strawberries and refrigerate at least 3 hours.

Yield 6–8 servings

Graham Cracker Crust

1 1/2	cups graham crackers, crushed
1/3	cup butter or margarine, melted
1/4	cup sugar

Pour graham cracker crumbs and sugar into a 9" pie pan. Add butter and blend together. Press mixture firmly into the bottom and up the sides of pan. Bake for 6 to 8 minutes at 350°. Cool, then fill.

Yield: One 9" crust

MOCHA TORTE

3   *cups sugar*
3   *eggs*
1/2   *cup butter*
3   *cups flour*
1   *tablespoon baking powder*
1   *cup strong coffee*
    fresh berries

Combine sugar and eggs in mixing bowl and beat until fluffy and blended. Add butter, flour, and baking powder; beat well, gradually adding coffee while mixing. Pour into a greased and floured bundt pan. Bake at 325° for 35 minutes. Remove and cool.

COFFEE FILLING AND ICING:

1   *can (14 ounces) sweetened condensed milk*
1 1/3 *cups butter*
1   *teaspoon coffee liqueur*

Combine the condensed milk, butter, and coffee liqueur and beat for 4 minutes. Cut cake into two horizontal layers, and spread 1/3 of filling over bottom layer. Top with second cake layer, and spread rest of filling on top and sides. Garnish with fruit, if desired.

Yield: 6–8 servings

DID YOU KNOW?

Coffee was brought to the New World (Martinique) in the early 18th century by a French naval officer by the name of deClieu, who smuggled a few tiny plants aboard his ship. It was a rough voyage; provisions were depleted rapidly, including the supply of drinking water. All but one of the coffee plants died enroute, thanks to an irate passenger who, begrudging the water they required, destroyed them. The Frenchman stood guard over the plant, shared his water ration with it, and it became the basis for the coffee industry in the Caribbean and South America.

ESPECIALLY FOR ENTERTAINING

How to Conduct a Coffee Tasting At Home

Theme parties are always popular and coffee tastings are the perfect opportunity to express your entertaining savvy. So many occasions are appropriate for hosting a coffee tasting, and you don't have to worry about a specific time of day.

Here are a few tips to help you get organized in putting together your own coffee tasting. But, these are just guidelines—be creative.

Supplies

1. Offer no more than six different coffees. You may use less. Here is the typical regimen:
   - Straight Coffee
   - Blend
   - Flavored
   - Decaffeinated
   - French Roast
   - Espresso
2. Use as many electric coffee makers as you have coffee.
3. Have six cups for each guest.

4. Offer spoons, cream and sugar (coffee should be tasted black but be prepared for this request).

5. Set out a coffee grinder

6. Serve accompaniments such as croissants, fancy cookies, crackers and cheese, baking soda breads, muffins or teacakes. Serve three or four different kinds. Don't serve gooey or sweet pastries. The abundant sugar may imbalance the flavor of the coffees.

7. Setup card or folding tables set up "coffee house" style. You may even want to use TV trays if there aren't many guests and you plan to use demitasse cups.

THE PROGRAM

A specialty coffee merchant can provide you with information about the coffees you have chosen—or might be willing to make the presentation personally at your home.

Describe the coffees you have selected, noting the size, shape, and roast of the beans. Grind and measure the coffee as recommended for each coffeemaker. You can choose to brew one coffee at a time or several at once. While the coffee brews, give a more detailed account of the coffee beans, countries of origin, grades, taste characteristics, history and lore. Ask guests to make note of the different aroma and taste characteristics as the coffees are sampled. Allow plenty of time to sip each coffee and to discuss its qualities. More than anything, enjoy, have a good time, and encourage your guests to participate.

Cold Drink Coffee Bar

On a long, cloth-covered table, arrange an array of garnishes in an assortment of unusual bowls, baskets, cream pitchers or relish plates. Fill a very large bowl with crushed ice, and "bury" serving glasses or mugs upside down. Put out ice cream scoops, long-handled spoons and straws, coasters and napkins. Place ice cream cartons on a bed of ice in a freezer chest, and brew several different coffees ahead of time and chill. At serving time, put coffees in carafes or pitchers.

For card-playing afternoons or summer Sunday get-togethers, have on hand:

Ice creams:		**Liqueurs:**	
	chocolate mint		Amaretto
	coffee		Cherry Heering
	vanilla		Cognac
	raspberry		Fruit Brandies
	banana		Creme de Menthe
	chocolate		Grand Marnier
	butter pecan, etc.		Kahlua

Garnishes: Whipped cream, chocolate shavings, nuts, cherries, nutmeg, fresh berries, cinnamon, peppermint candy canes, fancy chocolate "straws," circles of whole orange, pineapple spears, etc.

For each drink, put 1–2 scoops ice cream (vary flavors) and 2 tablespoons liqueur in tall glass or mug. Fill with coffee and garnish as desired.

For non-alcoholic drinks, substitute ⅛ teaspoon of flavor extract for liqueur (see Appendix for list, or use what you have on hand).

Hot Drink Coffee Bar

Cover and decorate your table. Arrange a variety of coffee cups—mugs, demitasse, café au lait—at one end. If you have an electric espresso machine, set it up on the table, or borrow a hot plate for your stove-top espresso maker*.

Fill a silver, crystal, or earthenware pitcher with fresh water. Use small, colorful baskets to hold an assortment of whole coffee beans-including some decaffeinated—(label if desired), and place on the table in a circle with your coffee grinder in the middle, and one or more coffee measures close by.

On a silver tray place a selection of bottles of liqueurs, and a jigger or two for measuring, and set up some liqueur glasses and brandy snifters "just in case." A vacuum pitcher of hot, bubbly milk (or a saucepan of milk kept hot on the stove) should be available. Arrange a cream pitcher and sugar bowl—use lumps of sugar for a change—sugar tongs, and demitasse and teaspoons on a small wooden tray so it can be passed around if necessary.

Choose some unusual ways to present garnishes (see Cold Drink Coffee Bar). If desired, save a place on the table for your blender (make coffee ice cubes ahead and place in an ice bucket) so you can offer a cold drink alternative.

Have guests select and grind their own coffee beans, and show them how to brew the coffee. As they wait, suggest some hot drink combinations:

> demitasse espresso with a lemon twist
>
> demitasse with liqueur added or on the side
>
> café au lait—half espresso/half hot milk, sugar to taste
>
> café au lait with liqueur
>
> cappuccino—half espresso/half hot milk, whipped cream and cinnamon, sugar to taste, etc.

As always, flavor extracts can be substituted for liqueurs (see Liqueurs and Extract Substitutions in Appendix).

*If you don't have an espresso coffee maker, brew extra-strong coffee a little ahead of time and hold in one or more vacuum pitchers.

Taco Bar

Put all ingredients in serving dishes so that your guests can make their own tacos. Suggest that they put cheese into their pita bread or taco shells first, so the hot meat will warm the cheese. Top with vegetables and hot sauce—more cheese, if desired. You will need:

Taco shells, warmed

Pita bread, slit (or halved) and warmed

Ground beef, cooked, seasoned and kept warm

Chicken, cooked, shredded and seasoned

Refried beans (mix in a little taco sauce and cheese as heated)

Cheddar or Monterey Jack cheese, shredded

Tomatoes, chopped

Onions, chopped

Avocado, sliced

Radishes, ripe olives, and anything else you choose

Taco sauce with coffee concentrate*

Sour cream and chopped green chilis

*Add ½ teaspoon coffee concentrate to each 1 cup of your favorite taco sauce, and stir well. The coffee adds pungency to any sauce you prefer.

Espresso Bar

Have on hand:
Demitasse cups and spoons
Mini ice cream scoops

Ice creams:
chocolate chip
strawberry
pistachio
fruit sherbets
Italian ices

Assorted brewed double-strength coffees, hot or chilled

A few hours in advance, brew coffees. If desired, chill them in small glass pitchers or carafes. If you wish to serve them hot, store freshly brewed coffees in thermal jugs. Label the coffee containers. To serve, place a tiny scoop of ice cream in each demitasse cup, then pour coffee over it. Enjoy!

APPENDIX

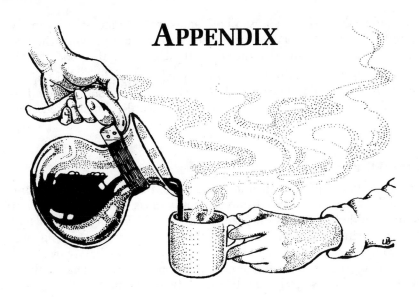

COFFEE BREWING

DRIP METHOD

This popular method of brewing most often uses a disposable paper filter into which the coffee is measured. Very hot 195–200° water is poured over the grounds, and drips into a glass carafe, and this is referred to as a "pour-over" brewing system.

Electric or automatic filter drip coffeemakers also employ the drip method, and offer the convenience of holding the coffee on a warming plate.

ESPRESSO MACHINES

"Espresso" means fast, and this method of brewing involves forcing steam and hot water, under pressure, through the dark-roasted finely ground coffee. Espresso coffee is enjoying great popularity, especially in cappuccino-like concoctions that are chosen more and more by diners in restaurants after dinner. While the brew is very tasty— whether served in demitasse or topped with cream and cinnamon—in practical terms, the one-cup-at-a-time aspect of this system might be considered a drawback, even though purists applaud it.

Stove-top versions of espresso coffeemakers are marketed by many manufacturers in 2 to 9 demitasse-sized cup capacities. While they do not produce a true espresso, the coffee they brew is quite good.

Electric espresso machines come as lavish—gleaming with copper and brass—or as simple as you like. A steam infuser should be a feature of the one you buy. They brew one or two demitasse-sized cups at a time.

COFFEE PRESSES

The experts are just about unanimous that this is the best brewing method. Coffee is measured into an empty glass carafe, and very hot water is added. After several minutes a plunger with a fine filter that fits snugly into the carafe is pushed through the brew to trap the coffee grounds at the bottom. The coffee is served immediately or stored in a coffee saver, since the grounds cannot be removed. The resulting brew is very rich, slightly cloudy, but truly excellent.

TURKISH COFFEE

The "original" brewing process, Turkish coffee is made in an *ibrik,* in which coffee, sugar, and water are boiled together over direct heat, resulting in a "muddy" concoction. When served in tiny cups, the mixture is foamy. The foam is called the "face" of the coffee, and is ceremoniously divided among the cups. You lose face if you serve Turkish coffee without the foam. The mud sinks to the bottom of the cup, so each serving amounts to only a few swallows. The brew is dark, thick, and intensely strong.

VACUUM

No longer widely used, but once considered a superior process of brewing coffee, the vacuum method was available in stove-top and electric versions. Reminiscent of a chemist's apparatus, water was measured into the lower bowl and brought to a boil. Fine-grind coffee was placed in the upper bowl, and when water was boiling, the upper bowl was inserted over the lower bowl and the hot water rose through the tube, mingling with the coffee, After a few stirs and a minute to steep, the coffeemaker was removed from its heat source. In another two minutes, the brewed coffee passed back through a permanent filter and down the tube into the lower bowl, leaving the grounds on top.

PERCOLATORS

The cardinal rule about brewing coffee is not to boil it or re-use the grounds. Percolators do both whether they are on the stove or electric. They brew the worst of all coffee and boil out the aromas. You deserve better.

COLD WATER BREWERS

It is possible to prepare a coffee concentrate by using one of the cold-water brewing devices currently available, in which freshly ground coffee is allowed to infuse in cold water for several hours, then filtered and stored in the refrigerator. The result is a liquid instant coffee that can be added to foods to lend flavor, or reconstituted with very hot water for drinking purposes. You may find its taste acceptable or you may prefer more traditional brewing methods.

VIETNAMESE COFFEE

A typical Vietnamese coffee brewer would involve a single-serve, lidded, stainless steel filter apparatus (check it out at your local specialty coffee supplier). The ground, French roast coffee is placed in the filter, hot water is added, and the lid—intended to preserve the aroma until the precise moment of consumption—is applied. The presentation is quite charming with each guest receiving an individual coffee brewer. Traditionally, the Vietnamese will add condensed milk to the brew, resulting in a very rich, exceedingly fragrant, and intensely sweet after dinner drink.

COFFEE ACCESSORIES

COFFEE CARAFES

Coffee connoisseurs never keep their coffee hot for hours or re-heat it. But most of us—whether at home or at the office—like the convenience of refilling our cups at will. Coffee carafes are the answer. Insulated, vacuum-type containers can be filled with freshly brewed coffee and will keep it hot for hours, without sacrificing quality. An added plus is their portability, allowing you to take your coffee wherever you like. The best thermal servers have air-tight stoppers; some employ a pump mechanism for serving, others must be partially unscrewed to pour. Previously found mostly in specialty stores, they are now widely available.

AIR-TIGHT CONTAINERS

We cannot stress enough the importance of storing coffee beans in air-tight containers in a cupboard or other dark place (current opinion has it that freezer storage leaches flavor from the beans). Your specialty coffee retailer can show you a variety of glass, ceramic, or porcelain jars that are fitted with a rubber seal and metal clamp closure to lock in freshness.

GRINDERS AND MILLS

Whether you buy a blend of coffee beans suggested by a retailer or choose your own, it is best to grind the beans at home, as you need them, storing the beans in an air-tight container in a cupboard or other dark place. There are many choices available, electric or manual; some with fine, medium, or coarse grind options; some without.

JAVA JIVE
ESPRESSO GLOSSARY

Americano—Espresso cut with hot water.

Breve—Latte made with steamed half-and-half.

Café au Lait—French version of the Italian caffè latte, similar beverages.

Caffè Latte—Espresso with steamed milk.

Cappuccino—Espresso with less steamed milk than a latte, topped with thick milk foam.

Con Panna—Espresso topped with whipped cream.

Crema—The dense, golden foam that is fresh espresso.

Double No Fun—A latte made with nonfat milk and a double shot of decaf espresso.

Double Tall Whipless—A tall mocha with a double shot of espresso and no whipped cream.

Espresso—Beverage, and brewing method, for coffee using pressurized hot water to extract the full flavor of the bean. Also means "quick."

Latteccino—a caffè latte with the milk texture somewhere between a latte and a cappuccino.

Lungo—The espresso shot is pulled "long," with additional water.

Macchiato—Espresso "marked" with a dollop of milk foam.

Mocha—Steamed chocolate milk poured over espresso.

No fun—A latte with decaf espresso.

Quad Tall Whipless Foamless—A rare flightless bird usually seen only after drinking a quad espresso.

Ristretto—Your espresso shot pulled short. Literally, "restricted" to the most flavorful part of the pour.

Short "A" With Room—Eight-ounce Americano with room for cream.

Tall Skinny—A tall latte made with nonfat or 1 per cent milk.

Tall Two—A tall latte made with 2 per cent milk.

LIQUEURS, ALCOHOL AND EXTRACTS

FLAVOR	LIQUEUR	SUBSTITUTE
Almond	Amaretto	almond extract
Almond/Hazelnut	Creme de Noyaux	almond extract
Apricot	Apricot brandy	
Banana		banana extract
Black Walnut		black walnut extract
Black Currant	Creme de Cassis	
Brandy	Various	brandy extract
Butterscotch		butterscotch extract
Cherry	Cherry Heering	cherry extract
Chocolate	Creme de Cacao	chocolate extract
Cinnamon		cinnamon extract
Coconut		coconut extract
Coffee	Kahlua & Tia Maria	coffee concentrate
Lemon		lemon extract
Licorice	Anisette	
Maple		maple extract
Orange	Grand Marnier	orange extract
	Cointreau	
	Triple Sec	
Peach	Peach Liqueur	
Peppermint/Mint	Creme de Menthe	peppermint extract
Pineapple		pineapple extract
Raspberry	Framberry	raspberry extract
Root Beer		root beer extract
Rum	Various	rum extract
Vanilla	Creme de Vanille	vanilla extract

Note: Substituting extracts for liqueurs will not, of course, result in an identical flavor, but combining brandy extract with, for example, chocolate or raspberry or orange extract should approach the desired result if you wish to avoid the alcohol.

Where It's Grown

The following countries grow an excellent variety of arabica coffees that are sold through specialty coffee and tea retailers as well as fine food sections of major department stores. Like many international commodities, availability varies according to prevailing economic conditions.

South America

Brazil   Santos is an excellent, medium bodied coffee. This sweet, widely used coffee is often used in blends. Except for Santos, most of the coffee grown in Brazil is arabicas, used in commercial blends.

Colombia   Supremo and Excelso are two top grades of this most famous coffee. Flavor is creamy, full-bodied with a satisfying aroma.

Venezuela   Low in acid, this light bodied coffee is widely used in blends. Often referred to as Maracaibo.

Central America

Mexico   Coatepec, Oaxaca Pluma, Altura (grown over 4,000 ft.) are all excellent. Fragrant, light-bodied, with a brisk snap that is pleasing to the palate.

Guatemala   Antigua and Coban are excellent choices. Taste is sharp and spicy, full-bodied, and good acidity. A favorite among those who work in the coffee industry.

Costa Rica   Tarrazu and others labeled Strictly Hard Bean are tops. A medium bodied coffee with tangy aroma offers cup after cup of complete satisfaction. This coffee offers a taste to match its wonderful aroma.

El Salvador Good for blending. Has a mild, sweet taste.

The Caribbean

Jamaica   Blue Mountain is the most expensive coffee in the world, and is available both pure and blended. Referred to as the "champagne of coffees," the taste is mild, extremely smooth, almost sweet. Two other excellent coffees from Jamaica are High Grown and Prime Washed; both may be marketed under different names.

ASIA

Java   Spicy, pungent aroma that offers a smooth, rich taste with low acidity. A partner with Mocha from Yemen or a fine Ethiopian coffee often marketed as a "mocha or mocca."

Timor   Rich, heavy body, the taste is definitely for the discerning palate.

Sumatra   Heavy, full body with slightly herbal aroma.

Celebes   Kalossi offers a rich aromatic full-bodied cup with relatively low acid. An impressive coffee to serve dinner guests.

Yemen   Mocha is the rare coffee associated with this region in Saudi Arabia. Mocha is named after a port from where it used to be exported. However, today, Mocha coffee is exported from Aden, another port in Yemen. Mocha is rich with a distinctive, fragrant aroma. Contrary to assumption, this coffee does not taste like chocolate.

UNITED STATES

Hawaii   Kona, the only coffee grown in the United States is mellow, smooth with a nutty aftertaste. Its medium body makes it easy to enjoy cup after cup. Kona is probably the most fragrant of all coffees and is available in 100 percent Kona as well as Kona blends.

AFRICA

Kenya   AA is the best. It is mellow, with decisive character and definite flavor.

Tanzania When you think of African coffee, this one offers the characteristic winy after-taste that makes this wonderful bean so memorable. Kilimanjaro is one of the best!

Ethiopia Harrar offers the exotic, sharp, earthy qualities so satisfying to connoisseurs. When Yemen Mocha is not available, this coffee is often substituted in the classic Mocha-Java blend.

Supplementary Reading List

For additional information about coffee, try your local library or book store for the following titles:

The Pocket Guide to Coffees & Teas by Kenneth Anderson, Putnam Publishing Group, 1982.

A Gourmet's Guide to Coffee & Tea by Leslie Mackley, Price Stern, 1989.

Coffee by Claudia Roden, Viking Penguin, 1981.

The Book of Coffee & Tea by Joel Schapira, St. Martin's Press, 1982.

Coffee by Violet Schafer and Charles Schafer, distributed by Random House, 1976.

The Perfect Cup, Coffee Lover's Guide to Buying, Brewing, & Tasting by Timothy James Castle, Addison-Wesley, 1991.

Café Olé Magazine, Wordsmith Publishing, 150 Nickerson Street, Suite 201, Seattle, WA 98109, (206) 217–9773.

Fresh Cup Magazine, Fresh Cup Publishing, P.O. Box 82817, Portland, OR 97282–0817, (503) 224–8544.